KU-092-195

Communicating Today

Television

Chris Oxlade

Heinemann
LIBRARY

www.heinemann.co.uk/library
Visit our website to find out more information about **Heinemann Library** books.

To order:
 Phone ++44 (0)1865 888066
 Send a fax to ++44 (0)1865 314091
 Visit the Heinemann Bookshop at www.heinemann.co.uk/library to browse our catalogue and order online.

First published in Great Britain by Heinemann Library, Halley Court, Jordan Hill, Oxford OX2 8EJ, a division of Reed Educational and Professional Publishing Ltd. Heinemann is a registered trademark of Reed Educational & Professional Publishing Ltd.

OXFORD MELBOURNE AUCKLAND JOHANNESBURG BLANTYRE
GABORONE IBADAN PORTSMOUTH NH (USA) CHICAGO

© Reed Educational and Professional Publishing Ltd 2001
The moral right of the proprietor has been asserted.

All rights reserved. No part of this publication may be reproduced, stored in a retrieval system, or transmitted in any form or by any means, electronic, mechanical, photocopying, recording, or otherwise without either the prior written permission of the Publishers or a licence permitting restricted copying in the United Kingdom issued by the Copyright Licensing Agency Ltd, 90 Tottenham Court Road, London W1P 0LP.

Designed by Visual Image
Originated by Ambassador Litho Ltd.
Printed in Hong Kong/China

05 04 03 02 01
10 9 8 7 6 5 4 3 2 1
ISBN 0431 11372 6

British Library Cataloguing in Publication Data

Oxlade, Chris
   Television. – (Communicating today)
   1. Television – Juvenile literature
   I. Title
   621.3'88

DUDLEY PUBLIC LIBRARIES

L   45770

627466   SCH

J621.388

Acknowledgements

The Publishers would like to thank the following for permission to reproduce photographs:
Associated Press: pp14, 27; Bush Internet: p26; Corbis: pp5, 8, 17, 20, 22, 28; David Hoffman: p19; Hulton Getty: p29; Liz Eddison: p12; Norman Osborne: p18; Pearson TV: pp7, 13, 18; R.D. Battersby: p24; Robert Harding: p11; Science Photo Library: p21; Sky News: p23; Sky, ABC, BBC, ITN: p6; Sony: p10; Stone: p15, Elie Bernager p4, Bob Thomas p9.

Cover photograph reproduced with permission of Stone.

Every effort has been made to contact copyright holders of any material reproduced in this book. Any omissions will be rectified in subsequent printings if notice is given to the Publisher.

CONTENTS

Any words appearing in the text in bold, **like this**, are explained in the Glossary.

COMMUNICATIONS

Communications are ways of sending and receiving information. Important ones include television, radio, telephone (and fax), the **Internet** (and **e-mail**), post and newspapers.

This book is about television. It examines how the television programmes that we watch are made and **broadcast**, the technology used and the people involved.

What is television?

A television system is one that makes moving pictures of a scene appear on a screen somewhere else, which might be very close to the original scene or thousands of kilometres away. The sounds made at the scene can also be heard through **loudspeakers** next to the screen. When we watch television, we are seeing pictures that are broadcast from television stations. This means that anybody with a television **receiver** can watch the pictures.

These children are watching television – one of the most popular pastimes in the world.

Only a few of the people who work in the television industry actually appear on our television screens. People with many different skills, such as camera operators and **floor managers**, work 'behind the scenes' in the making of programmes.

Television brings us a wide range of entertainment and information programmes, such as dramas, cartoons, comedies, sports events and game shows, news programmes and documentaries. Television news programmes are especially important. News **round-ups** and bulletins (short news summaries), and special news-only channels, bring pictures of events around the world to our homes, often **live** as they happen.

As well as explaining how a television works, this book will show you how some typical television programmes are made, presented, **transmitted** and watched. It also looks at how a typical news story is reported by a television station.

TELEVISION BROADCASTING

Television broadcasting is the process of making television programmes (consisting of pictures and sounds) and **transmitting** them so that anybody with a television **receiver** (usually called a television or television set) can watch them.

All television programmes, from news programmes to game shows, are made up of a collection of moving images and sounds. These might include presenters talking **live** into cameras and microphones, recorded images of people, places and events, programme **titles** and so on.

Stations and channels

There are thousands of television stations around the world. Some stations specialize in certain programmes, such as news, general entertainment, sport, documentaries or movies. Many stations **broadcast** several different channels at the same time, with each channel showing a certain type of programme.

Each television station has its own special logo. Many stations display a small logo on their pictures all the time so you can tell instantly which channel you are watching.

These people are planning a television programme. This is a complex job for programmes such as drama series that need to be filmed in advance and on location.

Some stations broadcast locally, others nationally, and some internationally. National stations are often broadcast from several different local television studios. This allows local programmes to be broadcast on the same channel.

Some television stations, such as the BBC in the UK, are paid for by public money, but most are commercial. This means they are funded by businesses, who pay to have their advertisements broadcast, or by users who **subscribe** to the channel, or both.

Pictures to the viewers

The first stage in making a television programme is organizing the programme's contents. Planning often begins weeks before the programme is due to be broadcast. The programme **scripts** have to be written. Presenters, camera crews and equipment need to be booked. Audiences and guests may also have to be invited. For outdoor filming, it may be necessary to order and build camera platforms.

When the programme is broadcast, the pictures and sounds are converted into electrical **signals** and sent to a television **transmitter**, which sends the signals across the country. Television receivers detect the signals and turn them back into the original pictures and sounds, which means that people like you can watch your favourite programmes.

GATHERING THE NEWS

The scene in the newsroom of a busy international television station. The journalists have to work quickly so that viewers get news of events almost as they happen.

Many television stations **broadcast** general entertainment programmes and a half-hour evening news **round-up**, as well as five-minute news bulletins, shown regularly during the day. Gathering the news stories for these programmes is the job of the journalists who work in the television station's newsroom.

In the newsroom

At a national television station there may be dozens of journalists working in the newsroom, including reporters, news **editors** (one each for general news, politics, sport, business and so on) and newsreaders.

News of events happening locally, nationally and internationally arrive in the newsroom all the time. It comes from the station's own reporters, **freelance** reporters, **press releases** and news agencies. A news agency, such as the famous Reuter's agency, is an organization that collects and writes news stories and sends them to any organization that **subscribes** to the agency.

At the scene of a news story, a reporter describes the events to the viewers, and interviews the people involved. The reporter often has to think fast while making live reports.

News reporters

The news editors decide which stories they want to show on the news programmes and choose reporters to investigate them. In the newsroom, reporters try to find more information about the stories. They might also go to the scene with a camera crew, to record interviews and make reports.

Most camera crews use a lightweight, but high-quality video camera with built-in recording equipment. Sound is sometimes recorded by the camera, and sometimes on a separate tape machine. Some crews also carry portable lighting equipment.

For example, news of a major flood might arrive in a newsroom in the middle of the day. A reporter will drive to the scene with a camera crew. He or she might record interviews with people whose homes have been flooded. The camera crew will also film scenes of the flood. Meanwhile, in the newsroom, another reporter or editor might arrange for experts to be interviewed, and perhaps for the station's weather forecaster to do a special report on the weather that caused the flood.

TELEVISION CAMERAS

When you watch television, you are actually seeing still pictures, displayed one after the other at a very fast rate. Depending on the system, there are either 25 or 30 pictures (called frames) a second. At this speed, your eyes cannot see the pictures changing. Instead you see a moving picture. The job of a television camera is to take these electronic pictures.

Two main types of camera are used in television. Studio cameras are large and heavy, but produce very high quality pictures. Lightweight video cameras are used by camera crews on the move or by roving camera operators in a studio.

Detecting light

At the front of a television camera is a lens. This collects light coming from a scene and focuses it on to a flat surface to create a small copy of the scene, called an image. This is where film in a normal camera would be. Electronic circuits **scan** the image from top to bottom, dividing it into hundreds of very thin horizontal lines called scan lines. They detect how much light from the scene is hitting each part of each line.

Television studio cameras can be mounted on tripods to make them stable while filming a programme.

Most television cameras work in colour. They use transparent coloured filters to divide the light from the scene into its red, blue and green parts. An image is made and scanned for each part.

Signals for pictures

The camera uses information from the scanning to control the strength of an electric current, so that the current is stronger where more light hits and weaker where less light hits. This changing current is called an electrical **signal**.

In this way, a television camera creates a continuous electrical signal that represents how much red, blue and green light there is along each scan line of an image, for one image after another. The signal represents a moving colour image, which can be **broadcast** at the time or recorded.

This is the view that a camera operator sees. He or she has controls for focusing and zooming in and out, and a screen that shows the picture the camera is producing.

RECORDING AND EDITING

For **live** programmes, such as an outside **broadcast** or studio discussion, the pictures from a television camera are broadcast straight to television **receivers**, where they appear instantly. But for many programmes, including parts of a news **round-up**, the pictures are recorded to be broadcast later. For example, at the scene of a fire, a report and interview would be recorded in the afternoon to be included in the evening news programme.

Tapes and disks

To record a picture, the **signal** from the camera is turned into a form that can be stored. To be stored on video tape, the signal is used to create a magnetic pattern in the magnetic coating on the tape. Modern cameras store the signals in **digital** form, which uses a combination of the digits 0 and 1. Digital signals can be copied again and again without losing quality, can be stored in computer memory or on disk, and are easily **edited**.

A camera operator filming with a lightweight, broadcast-quality digital video camera. The pictures can be stored on digital cassette in the camera or fed along a **cable** for live broadcast.

The lightweight camera used by film crews is a digital camera that stores pictures on digital tape in the camera itself. Studio cameras use separate recording machines to record signals.

Editing

Tapes from a reporter are usually sent back to the newsroom on a despatch bike. The reporter and crew normally record far more material than is needed, so an editor cuts it down to last for the correct amount of time.

A reporter decides what parts to include and helps the picture editor to edit the tapes. The reporter also adds some **voice-over** sound, such as descriptions of the flood. He or she might also write words (called copy) for the newsreader to read.

An editing suite at a television station. Here, pieces of recorded tape are cut and joined to make the final pictures that we see on our screens.

TELEVISION STUDIOS

Many television programmes, such as discussion programmes and game shows, are filmed entirely at television stations in huge indoor spaces called television studios. At most television stations the news studio is a dedicated studio, which means it only **broadcasts** news programmes. Other studios might be used for several different programmes, with sets that are dismantled after the programmes have been made.

Studio equipment

A typical studio contains television cameras and microphones for filming and detecting sounds, and lighting equipment. Each camera has a device called an **autocue** that displays the presenter's **script** and enables him or her to read it while looking into the camera. Camera operators, sound and lighting engineers and **floor managers** also work in the studio.

This weather map exists only in the memory of a computer. It is put behind the presenter electronically. He is really standing in front of a plain blue screen.

A television studio control room. The bank of screens shows pictures from various studio cameras. On the desk are controls for selecting and mixing pictures for broadcast.

The control room

Cables take electrical **signals** from the cameras and microphones in the studio to a control room. Here, pictures from all the cameras appear on a bank of monitors, together with pictures from outside broadcasts and other studios. There are also machines that play video clips and programme **titles**, and those that generate computer graphics.

Computer graphics can do almost anything – from adding simple captions to camera pictures, to building complete virtual studios. A virtual studio is a studio that exists only in the memory of a computer, but it looks real. Pictures of presenters in a real studio, shot against a plain blue background, can be placed in the virtual studio. With computer graphics you can also turn pictures upside down or the wrong way round, or mould them into any shape.

The programme director chooses which picture the viewers will see and gives directions to the camera operators. It is the vision mixer's job to work controls that switch pictures from one to another (this is called cutting) or mix pictures together, and the sound mixer switches between different sources of sound.

BROADCASTING THE NEWS

Once the news has been gathered, the stories written and all the videos **edited**, a news programme can be **broadcast**. The running order for a typical programme is shown below. It shows at what time each segment of the programme starts, how long it lasts and who reads the **script** for it. A one-minute story about a flood goes in exactly seven minutes into the programme.

Reading copy

The copy, or words, that the newsreader reads is written very clearly so that it is easy to see from the **autocue**. For example, the figure 50,000,000 is written as 50 million to save the presenter trying to count the zeros. Words that need to be emphasized are written in italic type or underlined. Where time allows, the presenter always rehearses reading the copy for each news report before it is broadcast **live** to the public, especially if it contains foreign words or names.

Time (mins : secs)	Programme section
00.00	Opening music
00.30	News summary (newsreader)
03.30	Live news report (reporter)
05.00	Recorded advertisements
07.00	Recorded news report (reporter)
08.00	News in brief (newsreader)
09.00	News interview (newsreader)
11.00	Recorded advertisements
13.00	News summary (newsreader)
15.30	Sports news (sports reporter)
18.30	Recorded advertisements
20.00	Recorded news report (reporter)
23.00	News interview (newsreader)
25.00	Weather (weather presenter)
27.00	Headlines (newsreader)
29.30	**Credits**
30.00	Programme ends

In control

In the control room all the recorded packages (collections of video and sound elements), introduction sequences and advertisements are made ready to play (this is called cueing). Links are also set up with camera crews and other studios for live reports and interviews.

As the programme is broadcast, the director chooses which picture from the studio cameras to show. Using different cameras adds interest to the programme. The vision mixer follows the director's instructions and also selects live pictures from camera crews and other studios when they are needed.

The newsreader looks into the camera and reads from the autocue. He gets messages about what news story is next through an earpiece, a small microphone in his ear.

MAKING MORE PROGRAMMES

On these pages you can see how a typical game show and an outside **broadcast** from an athletics meeting are made. Pictures from the outside broadcast are shown **live**, but the game show is recorded so that it can be shown at a later date. These programmes need some different equipment from the news programme, and the game show is made in a theatre-like studio, with a studio audience watching.

Making a game show

In preparing a game show, introduction **scripts** are written for the presenter to read (without seeming to read!) at the start of the show, quiz questions have to be researched and written, contestants selected and audience members invited.

Changing the position of the camera up and down or from side to side, and zooming in to show close-ups, make programmes like this game show more interesting to watch.

A television van at a small-scale outside broadcast. On top of the van is a dish that beams pictures to a nearby communications tower, from where they are relayed to the television station.

The studio cameras stand on the studio floor. From there the camera operators can pan and tilt to see all parts of the studio, and zoom in on contestants and audience members. The presenter carries a **radio microphone** in order to move freely around the studio and talk to the contestants. There is also a boom microphone that is suspended on a long pole and can move over the audience while staying out of view of the cameras.

The programme is recorded, then **edited** to the correct length. **Titles** are added at the start and **credits** at the end. As with a news programme, advertisements must be ready to play in time for the actual broadcast.

Outside broadcasts

At a typical outside broadcast, such as an athletics meeting, several studio-style cameras are needed to cover the stadium, together with lightweight cameras for track-side reports and interviews. There will also be a small studio inside the stadium where the presenters work. **Signals** from the cameras are sent to a mini control room in an outside broadcast truck, where the programme director works. Signals from the control room are sent back to the television station from a portable **transmitter**, either direct or via **satellite**.

BROADCASTING PICTURES

The pictures from the cameras and recordings that will be **broadcast** are selected by a programme director. But how do these pictures get to the screen of your television set? Broadcasting means sending pictures out over a wide area so that they can be seen on any television **receiver** in the area. There are three main ways that **signals** get from television stations to receivers – these are **terrestrial**, **satellite** and **cable**. You can see how signals are broadcast on page 22 and how they are received on page 24.

Terrestrial television

In terrestrial television, the pictures are broadcast from the television station by **radio waves**. The radio waves are made by sending an electrical signal to a transmitting **aerial**, which then sends out radio waves in all directions. The radio waves are detected by the aerial of any television set that they reach. National television stations have a **network** of **transmitters** so that pictures can be received throughout the country.

A cable which will carry television pictures (and also telephone calls) to homes is fed into an underground pipe.

Satellite and cable

In satellite television, pictures are beamed to an orbiting satellite using microwaves. The satellite re-**transmits** the pictures, again using microwaves, over an area of the Earth's surface thousands of kilometres across. Satellite television systems have a dish-shaped aerial that collects the microwaves and passes them to the receiver.

In cable television, pictures are sent through a network of underground cables, either as electricity in electrical cables or as light in optical-fibre cables. Any television connected to the cable network can receive the pictures.

Closed-circuit television

Television is not just used for broadcasting TV programmes. In closed-circuit television (CCTV), the pictures from television cameras are fed directly to one television (called a monitor because it is not a complete television receiver). One important use of CCTV is in security. For example, shops have cameras around the store. Security guards watch the pictures and record anybody stealing items.

Satellites like this orbit the Earth sending television pictures and many other communications around the world.

SENDING SIGNALS

Here's how **radio waves** are used to **broadcast** a **signal** in **terrestrial** television. Microwaves for **satellite** television and electricity for **cable** television work in a similar way.

The picture and sound signals are combined together and sent from the station's control room to a radio **transmitter**. The radio waves from the transmitter are like a vehicle that carries the signals. In fact, they are called carrier waves. To make the carrier wave carry the picture and sound signal, the shape of the carrier wave is changed by the signal making it stronger or weaker, or increasing or decreasing its **frequency**. This process is called modulation.

Station frequencies

Signals from different channels are broadcast on carrier waves with slightly different frequencies. This means that they do not get mixed together and **receivers** can choose between them. When you press a button on your television remote control, the television tunes itself to collect the correct signals for the channel you want to watch.

A television transmitter mast. The transmitter itself is at the very top of the mast. This allows the transmitted signals to reach a wider area than if the transmitter were at ground level.

Analogue and digital television

Television signals are either analogue or **digital**. The strength or frequency of an analogue signal can have many different levels. In contrast the strength or frequency of a digital signal has only two levels, represented by the binary digits 0 and 1.

Digital television has two main advantages over analogue television. The first advantage is that digital signals suffer much less from interference from other radio waves than analogue signals. This interference can produce fuzzy or sparkly images, or extra ghost-like pictures on the television screen.

The second advantage is that digital signals need much smaller carrier waves, so far more channels can be broadcast. In fact, dozens of digital channels can be sent on the same carrier wave as one analogue signal.

Digital television allows television stations to offer extra on-screen services to viewers. This is a news channel that allows the viewer to choose which news to watch.

TELEVISION RECEIVERS

The job of a television **receiver** is to collect television **signals** and turn them into a moving picture and sound. Most televisions have in-built electronics that allow them to receive **terrestrial** television signals. To receive signals from **satellite** and **cable** stations, an extra 'set-top' box may be needed.

Aerials and tuning

Terrestrial and satellite television systems need an **aerial**. Terrestrial aerials are lengths or loops of wire; satellite aerials are dish-shaped. When signals hit the aerial, they create tiny electrical signals in the aerial. This signal is the same as the shaped carrier wave that was **transmitted**, but millions of times weaker. The receiver's tuning circuits collect carrier waves from the stations you want and ignore all the others.

The original picture and sound signals are removed from the carrier wave they came on, and amplified (made bigger). The sound signal goes to a **loudspeaker**.

The inside of a normal television set. The tube can be seen in the centre. It contains a vacuum so that the electrons can travel from the guns to the screen.

Rebuilding the picture

Most television sets contain a large glass tube, shaped like a broad-based vase. The screen is the base of the tube. Tiny guns in the neck of the tube fire beams of tiny particles called electrons at the screen. There is one beam each for the red, blue and green parts of the picture. Each beam hits tiny coloured dots on the back of the screen, making them glow.

The beams **scan** together across the back of the screen, working from top to bottom, rebuilding the lines of the picture frames taken by the camera. The picture signal controls the strength of each beam as it scans. The stronger the beam, the more the dots glow. So in a red part of a picture, the beam for red will be at full strength, and the beams for blue and green will be at minimum strength.

Flat-screen televisions do not have a picture tube. Instead the picture signal controls the brightness of tiny dots in a liquid crystal display, similar to that on an electronic calculator.

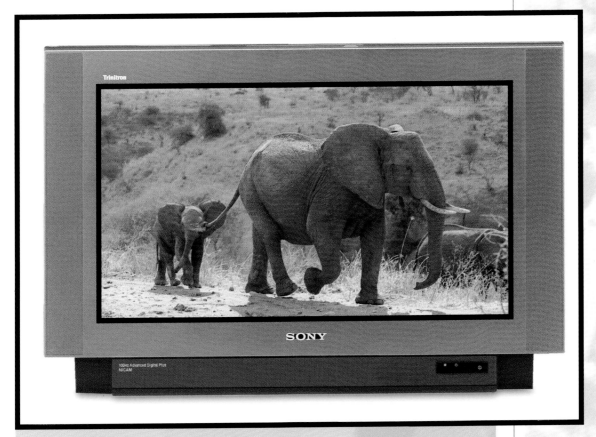

A flat, wide-screen television. A flat television has no tube, so it can be hung on the wall like a painting.

TELEVISION AND THE INTERNET

At the beginning of the 21st century, communications technology and the way we communicate are changing very quickly. This is known as the communications revolution. The main reasons for the changes are the development of **digital** communications and the growth of the **Internet**.

Convergence

In recent years, new inventions and developments in communications mean that a television set can do more than just receive and show television programmes. For example, some televisions can be used to view Internet web pages and send and receive **e-mails**. Many personal computers can receive television through an **aerial**, and computers with a high-speed connection to the Internet can show **live** television pictures (which is called netcasting rather than **broadcasting**).

It is now possible to use a television for more than just watching TV programmes. This girl has received an e-mail on her television.

People taking part in a video conference. Each person sits in front of a camera and can see all the other people on a screen, as though they were in the same room.

So different types of communications are becoming mixed together. This is known as convergence. By 2010, it is probable that all your communications will be sent and received through just one machine that will do the job of a television, a computer, a radio and a telephone.

Television on demand

The latest televisions contain a computer that will record digital programmes. They will also remember your viewing habits and record programmes that they think you might want to watch. It will also be possible to copy any programme ever made to your television to watch when you want.

Video-conferencing

A video-conferencing system allows people in different places to see and hear each other live on television or computer screen. The system needs small video cameras to take the pictures, and screens to display the pictures on.

TELEVISION TIMELINE

Here are some of the major events and technical developments in the history of television.

1864 British physicist James Clerk Maxwell predicts that **radio waves** exist.

1888 German physicist Heinrich Hertz proves that radio waves exist.

1884 In Germany, Paul Nipkow invents the Nipkow disc. This is a disc with a spiral pattern of holes in. When it is spun round, the holes divide the light from a scene into lines, acting as a crude mechanical camera.

1923 In the USA, Vladimir Zworykin invents the iconoscope, a glass tube that contains the electronics for taking moving pictures. It forms the heart of the first television cameras.

1926 British engineer John Logie Baird demonstrates a working television system in public for the first time. It has a mechanical camera and **receiver** based on the Nipkow disc.

1929 Experimental **broadcasts** using Baird's television system begin.

John Logie Baird's first public demonstration of a working television system in 1926. Compare the huge size of the cabinet with the tiny size of the screen (the round hole on the right).

1936 The first regular television broadcasts are started by the BBC in London. At first only a few hundred people have television sets.

1939 NBC begins regular broadcasts in the USA.

1953 Colour broadcasting begins in the USA.

1956 The first video recorder is developed by the Ampex Corporation in the USA. For the first time, programmes can be taped and broadcast again later. Before this, all studio programmes had been **live**.

1962 Television pictures are relayed across the Atlantic using radio **signals** by the Telstar communications **satellite**.

1989 Satellite television broadcasting begins in Britain and Europe.

1990s **Digital** television services begin.

1999 Televisions that can access the **Internet** and send and receive **e-mails** become widely available.

A television studio in Britain in 1953, the year colour broadcasting began in the USA. Compare the television camera on the right to the one on page 10.

GLOSSARY

aerial length of wire, metal rod or coil of wire that creates or detects radio waves

autocue device that attaches to the front of a television camera and displays words. It allows a presenter to read the words while looking into the camera.

broadcast 1) to transmit signals that television receivers can detect. 2) A programme that is transmitted.

cable 1) flexible pipe containing lengths of wire or optical-fibres. 2) A way of broadcasting by sending signals along cables.

credits list of people involved in making a programme, shown at the beginning (opening credits) or end (closing credits) of it

digital 1) signal that is made up of on and off pulses of electricity, represented by the digits 0 and 1. 2) Any information stored in the form of the binary digits 0 and 1.

e-mail short for electronic mail, a system that allows people to send written messages to each other's computers via the Internet. Also the name given to a message.

edit to cut out or move around words, pieces of sound or pictures until they read correctly or last for a required length of time

editor person who edits words, sounds or pictures, or decides what goes into a programme

floor manager supervisor who makes sure everything runs smoothly in the studio

freelance not employed by one company or organization, but working for several

frequency number of waves that pass a point every second

Internet global computer network that allows people with computers linked to it to access information on any other computer around the world, and to exchange e-mails with other people with computers

live sounds or pictures of events that are broadcast to television receivers as the events happen

loudspeaker device that turns an electrical signal that represents a sound back into sound

network chain of interconnected things, in this case transmitters

on location when a programme is filmed outside a studio, in the appropriate setting

press release information about an event or news story written and distributed by a person, company or organization

radio microphone type of microphone which uses radio waves to function and so does not have a cable attached to it

radio waves invisible electromagnetic waves that can pass through air and space

receiver short for television receiver, a device that detects radio waves that have been broadcast and turns them back into the pictures and sounds that came from the television station

round-up summary of all the latest news stories

satellite 1) object that orbits around the Earth in space. 2) System of broadcasting television pictures via satellites.

scan to cover an area by zig-zagging backwards and forwards across it in narrow lines

script written words for a presenter or newsreader to read

signal changing electric current, radio wave or beam of light that represents a moving picture or sound

subscribe to pay a monthly or yearly fee for a service

terrestrial system of broadcasting television pictures via aerials on the Earth's surface

titles opening pictures in a programme that give the programme's name, the name of the company that made it and so on

transmit to send out signals

transmitter aerial that sends out radio waves

voice-over commentary by an unseen speaker which is heard at the same time as pictures are seen

INDEX

Titles in the *Communicating Today* series:

Hardback   0 431 11375 0

Hardback   0 431 11370 X

Hardback   0 431 11374 2

Hardback   0 431 11371 8

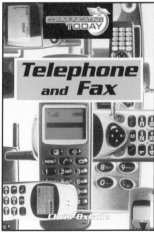

Hardback   0 431 11373 4

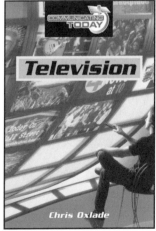

Hardback   0 431 11372 6

Find out about other Heinemann resources on our website www.heinemann.co.uk/library